Spending a Penny in Southwold

Sue Thompson

2020

First Edition

Published and Printed by

Leiston Press

Masterlord Industrial Estate

Leiston

Suffolk

IP16 4JD

Telephone Number: 01728 833003

Email: glenn@leistonpress.com

ISBN: 978-1-911311-73-7

Dedication

For Jon, Lucy and Kelly

Thank you for making our Sunday evenings so

special with your wonderful music

throughout lockdown.

Contents

Preface

Remember 2018 anyone, back in the days when we used to huddle close together in cosy pubs and complain about a few feet of snow? When a few months later we baked in the hottest summer on record? Well, this was the year I decided to have a long staycation in beautiful Suffolk whilst writing about all the glorious beaches, pretty villages and amazing food on offer in these parts, tempt the tourists to come in their hordes and spend all their money boosting the local economy.

It seemed like a good idea at the time although now I know I should have written faster, much faster, because it doesn't seem such a good idea any more.

Some of our local businesses will not survive the Covid pandemic and its economic consequences and others will evolve to provide new and exciting experiences for visitors to enjoy but for now tourism is a contentious point among Suffolk natives, especially with our current problems concerning litter, perilous parking and overcrowding.

A quiet hidden beach is becoming a precious rarity and certainly not something to be advertised.

I was considering binning my efforts when Suffolk Radio kindly started broadcasting my stories on their Upload slot, adding appropriate music and cleaning up the tinny sound produced when I recorded them on my Smartphone.

It was good to hear my musings on air, I was fond of them and didn't want them to go unpublished so I decided to put together a book of short stories aimed at amusing people in these very sombre times.

During lockdown I found myself constantly thinking of novel ways to keep myself occupied.

I needed to find new experiences that didn't involve spending half my life in the car roaming the lanes of Suffolk in search of fun times and calories.

I even wrote a few poems during my solitary walks, the rhythm of walking made words unexpectedly form in my head, the poems wrote themselves- and I lost weight! Brilliant.

I wanted to illustrate my new writings with pictures that reflected the feelings of peace and innocence produced by walking slowly down country lanes and I found this in the lovely sketches made by my friend and fellow Desperado, Lorraine Woolnough.

Apologies in advance for gently mocking some of the more well known Suffolk hotspots like Southwold and Aldeburgh. I am very fond of them really and wouldn't have them any other way, just wish they weren't so crowded and overpriced, especially in regard to public toilets!

Spending a Penny in

Southwold

Is it just me or does every holidaymaker arrive at their destination desperate for the loo? No matter how short your journey, or how strong your bladder, no sooner have you clunked your car door shut than you get an old familiar unwelcome feeling and have to set off at a trot for that dreaded unknown quality, the public toilet. Will it be open, will it be spidery, but I must admit that up until now, in lovely friendly Suffolk, I had never asked myself " How much will it cost?"

We first headed for the pier, knowing they had nice clean free loos, but the pier toilets were closed so we hurried on towards the ones on the beach, only to find using them would cost 20p. I find this a difficult concept to warm to, as my hero and fellow mean traveller Bill Bryson would say, especially as the machines in the Southwold inconveniences didn't give change.

Trying to think about anything but my swollen bladder, I headed into town to look for a bank to arm myself with enough 20ps to last me the day only to make the alarming discovery that the damn bank was closed on Tuesdays (of course we would pick a Tuesday to make our visit. Why Tuesday? How random is that?)

Southwold is a town which considers itself so desirable

it sells beach huts for £130,000, you would think the council could provide free loos, although maybe visitors to Southwold are so wealthy they just don't care.

Eventually we found some very posh free toilets in the Adnams cafe so I didn't have to wander the streets of Southwold in damp underwear and in future we will be better prepared.

On a brighter note, we did have a marvellous fish and chip lunch in the Beach Bistro cafe, a retro delight on the pier from which you could watch the monstrous waves crashing against the shoreline as you cosied up to your fellow diners (it is quite a bijou beach cafe but this is Suffolk and folks like to get up close to each other over a cup of tea and a pickled egg).

The tables here look as if they have been designed by those folk who make deck chair material, with day-glo striped vinyl reminiscent of the 1950's.

It is the sort of place you would expect to hear a recording of Elvis or Marty Wilde playing in the background to accompany the roar of the amusement arcade next door, but on the day we visited the radio was playing Pachelbel's Canon. Perhaps there is a committee in Southwold employed to ensure all music played in fish and chip shops conforms to Southwold standards.

We enjoyed Pachelbel's Canon, the last time we heard it was at our daughter's wedding in 2002 and it brought back lovely memories to go with the excellent fish and chips.

Orford tomorrow, I'm taking my piggy bank with me and doing some bladder control excercises.

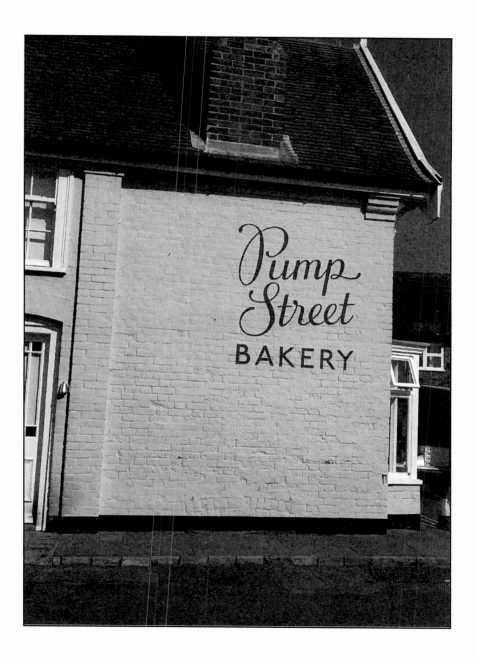

Eccles Cakes In Orford

Orford has a bit of a reputation in these parts for being a twee tourist destination with inadequate parking and overpriced eateries but our visits during the quiet winter months had been so enjoyable we decided to revisit during our present scorching summer.

My favourite place to eat in Orford by a mile is the Pumphouse Bakery on the square. It has a tiny intimate dining room consisting of one large table completely filling the sun-filled space, meaning you have no choice but to share your cups of tea and sticky buns with anyone who happens to be there already.

Don't be shy, this is Suffolk and it's quite normal to chat with strangers over an Earl Grey and an Eccles cake.

As we made ourselves comfortable we discovered our lunchtime companions weren't strangers at all but the very same holidaymakers we had met the previous day while exploring Southwold.

We bonded further over the loveliness of Orford with its freedom from overpriced toilets and extortionately priced beach huts, and then the conversation turned to the food on offer in the Pumphouse. Our new friends said they could highly recommend the Eccles cakes, we shouldn't leave without giving them a try.

Well we always love a foodie challenge so give them a

try we did and they were a revelation.

My previous experience of Eccles cakes had been hard flat sugar-crusted currant-strewn offerings, like edible Frisbees, and they were the good ones.

The Pumphouse Bakery version proved to be another animal altogether. Plump and moist in the middle due to being packed with currants, then flaky and buttery on the outside. They were huge but this did not stop us greedily ordering and wolfing down seconds to go with our Earl Grey.

Our Southwold friends told us that the currants were steeped in Armagnac prior to gracing our treats, which explained why despite the upper 30s temperature I found myself feeling Christmassy.

 I did briefly consider ordering a third but as I had already undone two buttons on my shorts I decided to call it quits and return another day wearing elasticated trousers.

Orford is well worth a visit, just not if you are on a diet!

Angry In Aldeburgh

Aldeburgh is recognised by those who care about such things as a centre of culture.

The small Suffolk seaside town was the home of the composer Benjamin Britten and was chosen as the setting for the international Alde Festival of the arts at nearby Snape Maltings.

Other festivals available near the town include the enormously popular food festival held at the end of September with demonstrations from local chefs on offer as well as opportunities to meet celebrity cooks and former bake-off contestants.

Last year we enjoyed a demonstration of Indian cooking by bake-off finalist Chetna Makan and an entertaining and informative talk by judge and famous cookery writer Prue Leith.

Also at the 2018 food festival we were delighted to find a wild Suffolk area where demonstrations showing different methods of cooking local game could be enjoyed while seated country style on straw bales. Chefs from the delightful Froize Inn at nearby Chillesford were on hand to guide you through the mysteries of prepping pigeons and partridges, or if you had doubts about your knife skills, as I have, you could buy these birds in pie form from Gloria the Froize mobile food wagon.

This event is not for slimmers!

Master classes were held over the weekend in lots of different venues where you could get hands-on with chocolate making or pasta , Indian Street Food, Vietnamese feasting and even sugar-free baking. Can't wait to see what's on offer next year.

There is also an annual poetry festival to enjoy and throughout the year a programme of classical concerts takes place in the fine auditorium at Snape Maltings. You would be advised to take a cushion along for these events as the chairs provided are notoriously uncomfortable.

The Aldeburgh festival of music and the arts takes place from the beginning June, also at the Snape concert hall. The events are very reasonably priced which makes for an ideal way to sample something new and different during your stay if you are holidaying in Suffolk.

 In the summer you can go along to the bandstage on the beach where local musicians can be discovered entertaining the crowds packed along the shore for free. Buy an ice cream and soak up the atmosphere, or grab some of Aldeburgh's famous fish and chips for a salty seaside treat.

We were expecting some sophisticated refinement and a better class of holiday-maker therefore when we pitched up on another heat-blasted day in August, but to our surprise the highbrow event on offer was a fight.

We were driving slowly down one of Aldeburgh's back roads searching optimistically for a parking space when we discovered some enterprising workmen busily painting one of the quaint old townhouses in a cute shade of beach-hut pastel.

They had sensibly blocked off the road to ensure the safety of the painter high on his ladder above the narrow street, and the fun began when the driver of a Norse van begged to differ on the wisdom of closing public roads in the interest of safety.

He wound down his window shouting that the barrier needed to be removed as he was coming through. Voices were raised and the parties involved then indulged in what the British Board of Film Certification would call "moderate swearing"

Oo-er missus!

We scarpered before things got out of hand, squeezed into what we hoped was a legal parking spot and went exploring, keeping a close watch for more Norse van drivers on the rampage.

We have some newcomers to Suffolk living on our estate who insist that Aldeburgh is really pronounced Aldi-Burgh, which I find delightful as it conjures up an image of streets lined with branches of Aldi painted in Farrow and Ball colours selling slightly battered boxes of Waitrose style food at extortionate prices.

We call it Aldi Burgh ourselves now and earn glares from

the august residents ofAldeburgh who think we should show more respect for their cultural status. At least we don't swear at their decorators.

Aldeburgh is rightly famous for its fish and chip shops, so as it was after our usual lunch time by now we were feeling excited at the prospect of large amounts of salty battered high calorie fare wrapped in newspaper (wouldn't that be nice). Strangely there seemed to be no queues outside the two popular chippys so blessing our luck we hurried along to be greeted with disaster. Both chippys were closed!!

What kind of sadist closes a chip shop at 2pm? It's still lunch time in Essex, in fact I don't think I have ever seen an Essex chippy closed, and that includes one I once visited at midnight after a long night at the Talk of the South(this was in the70s though and things might have changed).

I recently came across a new word "Hangry" to describe a person enraged by lack of food. Well, I now felt "Chumpy", grumpy through lack of chips. Perhaps Norse man had the same problem, it's enough to make you knock down bollards and splatter decorators across the pavement.

Cruelly denied our carb fest, we looked around for something tasty to sample in foodie Aldeburgh and discovered a tiny 50s style ice cream parlour called Ives . This delightful establishment offers a choice of around 30 flavours so that an ice cream lover such as myself could spend many happy moments browsing and changing her mind, but the queue was long and the temperature Saharan so I was forced to make my choice.

I opted for chocolate brownie (when in doubt go for the healthy option), but with an exciting and unexpected twist.

Ives is also a coffee shop and some enterprising genius had come up with the idea of offering a mini cone (I love miniature food) with a coffee for £2.70.

Hey presto, affogato! By 'eck it's posh in Aldi-burgh.

We perched outside on one of those trendy metal garden chairs that add instant chic. We bought a similar set complete with a little garden table last year at a bargain price from the auction rooms in nearby Campsea Ashe. When I found comparable ones on sale at the smart garden centre in Snape Maltings for a three figure sum it made my year.

Lounging on our trendy chairs outside Ives in the sunshine watching the Aldeburgh glitterati go by made us feel very hip and continental. Who needs chips?

To walk off the sugar rush we explored the back streets of Aldeburgh in the blast furnace heat, and discovered a sign on a cottage garden wall which read " Dartmouth", and a little further on came across another charming dwelling dubbed "Edinburgh Cottage".

So if you want some dodgy geography to go with your road rage, followed by a bespoke affogato, come to trendy Aldeburgh. It's full of surprises.

Fear and singing in the Peak District

Before you clever people reading this inform me that the Peak District is not in Suffolk, even someone as geographically confused as myself is aware of this, but I like this story and thought I would include it as an example of how to overcome, or at least live with, your limitations.

Back in 2005 my husband took early retirement and we used some of his pension money to buy a caravan. It had long been our dream to tour Britain slowly, stopping wherever we felt the need to explore, so we took off for nine weeks starting in early April and following the Spring as we travelled north.

 I discovered lots of unexpected things about myself, many of them challenging ones. I prefer to call them character-building although my poor husband says it is his character that was built during our excursions.

 Our walks in the Peak District proved adventurous in ways you really don't plan when packing for a country ramble, and this particular experience still haunts my dreams making me very glad we now live in Suffolk where the only wildlife we encounter are large herds of deer which tend to skeddadle at our approach.

Of course, the arrival of Covid 19 has given me plenty

of opportunities to add to my list of phobias: small children with coughs, people with loud voices who invade your personal space, nail bars, swimming pools and sweaty runners.

I have a recurring nightmare in which I take a wrong turning on the A14 and end up in Leicester, or Arizona (that's some wrong turning).At this rate I'll lose my fear of cows and spiders because there is simply no spare room in my brain.

I have many fears, many many fears...............

Heights, depths (it's a miracle I ever leave the house), spiders, lightening, creepy tree stumps, falling over, making a fool of myself and cows. The last and perhaps greatest of my fears became a big problem when my intrepid husband suggested we take a walking holiday in the Peak District, it would be fun, I would enjoy it. He had heard the weather was bracing, whatever that may mean. It turned out that bracing meant wet. If I had wanted a swimming holiday I would have chosen Barbados, or preferably stayed at home (I'm scared of water as well).

I think he picked the Peak District not for the bracing walks or the beauty of the scenery but out of spite or perhaps as a bad joke because the Peak District, or at least the parts of it we walked, is the cow capital of Great Britain. It's like Texas without the oilfields, or J R Ewing.

They hide, you know, cows, great hairy packs of them, only to jump out at you when you reach the point in their field furthest from the gate or a handy stile and there is no escape, they can see you and you're not getting out untrampled so you might as well just lie down and get it over with. No-one is coming to save you in all the wind and rain, should have stayed at home where you belonged.

We had, however, packed all our walking gear and rainproof clothing. The pair of us were buried under crackly layers of plastic designed to keep out the never ending deluge encountered on our spring odyssey through the walking destinations of Britain. There was no alternative, I would brave the fields full of terrifying beasties to prove my courage and for this I needed a strategy.

This consisted of pulling my raincoat hood over my head, because it's a well-known fact that if you can't see them they can't see you.

This worked as we went yomping across the fields waving our walking sticks boldly from side to side singing as we went ("I whistle a happy tune, so no-one will suspect I'm afraid". I sing this a lot. It keeps me calm).

In fact I felt perfectly safe and secure in my rain-proof cocoon until we reached a stile and removed our hoods to climb over it.

I had expected the cows to keep their distance as we were both invisible but no, only a few short feet from where we had been walking the herd had gathered. All of them. They were HUGE. I quickly replaced my rainhood and they disappeared again, back to the land of no-cows that is the default mode of my dream walkers world in which cows do not inhabit fields and bullocks certainly do not block your path when you have just trekked six miles to visit Ashford in the Water and are desperate for a cream tea...

This particular walk started so well, the rain stopped and we optimistically donned our smart new walking shorts and summer weight blister proof socks to celebrate the sudden dramatic rise in temperature into double figures.

On balance, if we had known what was in store for us at the end of our adventure we would have packed hand grenades and rubber bullets.

It was a lovely walk, the sun warmed our backs and the floods had subsided so we didn't need to ford every stream, we didn't get lost or have rows about which route we should be following and there were no unruly cows in the fields. Happy days indeed.

Towards the end of the walk, within the last half mile, just when the thighs were beginning to burn and visions of steaming teapots were tantalisingly within reach, an obstacle appeared completely blocking the path ahead.

It was a moving obstacle, swaying menacingly from side to side in familiar nightmare-inducing fashion. A barrier of black, glistening, threatening muscle and horn. Bullocks!

There must have been around twelve of the little beggars, jostling for position like members of a biker gang. It was bad enough seeing them in front of us but then they turned round slowly and regarded us with that bovine curiosity that can change from friendly greeting to murderous intent in a heartbeat.

They had that lively, skittish attitude healthy young animals display when they are bored and looking for mischief, or in this case sizing us up before trampling us into the ground for invading their patch.

As panic gripped I cast desperately around for an escape route and spotted a likely retreat into a densely wooded area, the problem being this wood was located behind a vertical bank overgrown with hawthorn bushes and gorse. This was the only available escape on offer so I threw myself up the bank using all the adrenalin now surging through my bullock-befuddled veins.

What actually happened was that I steamed straight up like an over-excited four year old then ran out of momentum, because I am no longer four, stopped dead, waved my arms desperately in the air as if this would help me to keep going, or even enable me to fly, then descended as rapidly as I had ascended, landing at the hooves of my nemesis.

A sharp intake of breath followed before I stopped breathing altogether, in fact I froze like one of those people you see in London pretending to be statues. Perhaps if I didn't move they wouldn't be able to see me, although I have already proved this doesn't work I cling to the hope that one day it will.

My husband suddenly came out of his trance, the one that he falls into when I do something he finds strange. Summoning up some manly courage he waved his walking stick at the gang and shouted " Shoo!".

The bullocks ignored him and continued to mill around us with that look of superior curiosity now tinged with excitement.

They were in the mood for some tourist-trampling fun.........

We needed a plan, and fast.

The choices were limited, we couldn't run as this might over stimulate the gang of twelve who could certainly out-run us, especially as I was still doing my best frozen statue impression.

Then there was the cowards' way out, the one we chose to adopt, turning slowly and quietly around, retracing our steps and tramping reluctantly back to our campsite six miles away. We followed the dreary path we had taken so optimistically several hours earlier, searching for tea and scones at one of the prettiest villages in the

Peak District according to our walkers guide.

We never did see Ashford in the Water, but I'm sure it's absurdly picturesque, in fact we later learned the village boasts the most photographed bridge in Great Britain, the famous Sheep Wash Bridge over the River Wye. It would have been a lovely picture to add to our memory book. Just not worth being mauled by bullocks for.

But I did get my revenge that evening when we headed out to a local restaurant and I ordered a nice big juicy steak........

Ipswich......Looking up and

falling down

This chapter is dedicated to all those brave souls who open independent shops in our towns and make visiting such a joy. Why use the horrible internet when you can speak to real people who share your passions and can advise and encourage you. If you are really lucky you can come away with an inspirational day to remember as we were fortunate enough to do. Go on, give it a try............

This morning I was listening to Radio Suffolk as usual when I heard an amusing story concerning our poor much maligned county town of Ipswich.

I had to quickly check the date when I learned the dear old place had been named as the only UK town listed by TripAdvisor as an emerging tourist destination.

Apparently our local hotspot is being bookmarked by the international glitterati for their forthcoming hols.

Ipswich? Our Ipswich? That well-known litter strewn capital of knife crime where decent shops are unknown and the police don extra Kevlar vests when boldly venturing from their patrol cars?

Some wit on the radio asked if the TripAdvisor people

meant Ipswich Australia (I didn't know there was another Ipswich, in Australia of all places, every day's a school day).

Someone else commented saying their favourite view of our county town was the one in their rear-view mirror as they sped away, which I thought was a tad harsh but still quite amusing.

Apparently Ipswich is now a globally recommended destination, which is sure to keep the residents of Paris and Barcelona up at night worrying about their prospects. Perhaps we should lend them Ed Sheeran......

As I needed to visit Ipswich that day (the eye department of the hospital, though not yet a tourist hot-spot they had made a lovely job of removing my cataracts) I decided to check out the attractions before the queues got too long and the prices went up.

Emerging from the park and ride at the stop opposite the Regent theatre (one example of the attractions mentioned is that Ipswich is blessed with many fine theatres and the Regent is certainly one of them) we strolled into town.

Unfortunately the first part of our walk didn't bode well with rows of shops closed and boarded up and many others displaying sad signs reading "Closing down, last days of sale".

This area was drab and unwelcoming although it wasn't

strewn with litter, in fact I was impressed throughout my visit with how clean the streets were. Well done to everyone responsible, it can't be easy keeping a large busy area such as Ipswich spick and span and it shows that someone cares.

Once we passed this run down part of town things improved and on raising my eyes from the boring new shop fronts to take in the roof line I stopped in amazement. Next time you find yourself in Ipswich do yourself a favour and look up, the view is gorgeous.

 Turrets and balconies worthy of Romeo and Juliet appear. Look at the Lloyds Avenue building with its graceful arches and smart red brickwork.

Then the beautiful stonework above W H Smith, such an arresting sight I took out my phone and photographed this unexpected loveliness while all around me folk scurried about their business probably unaware of what they were missing.

Where were the hordes of Japanese tourists with their expensive cameras and insatiable appetite for recording everything in sight? I wouldn't have been able to stop and film in Barcelona, I'd have been trampled underfoot.

Our reason for coming to Ipswich that day, apart from confirming that I now have 20/20 vision and checking out our unexpected new hotspot, was to sell my second book about the folk scene here in Suffolk to the music shops.

Did you know that Ipswich has three independent music shops: Music World, Rocket Music and West End Music? There may be more, but this was enough to make me very happy. This is my kinda town!

I heard recently that in March there will be a new indie bookshop opening in Dial Lane, another reason to visit and spent more money on books.

We visited the first two music shops on our list then set off for pastures new, West End Music.

One of the things I have learned in my long and interesting life is that if a person younger than you (this group has grown astonishingly large in the last few years) tells you somewhere isn't far, they are lying. If they say it will only take 10 minutes to get there they are lying through their perfect teeth.

We were advised to negotiate the underpass and West End Music would be nearby on the left. This should have rung alarm bells, we had never come across an underpass in Ipswich and had forgotten the directions given by our youthful new friend before we had covered 100 yards.

My husband is waiting for a second knee replacement and at present needs a stick to get around. The journey to the underpass took around 20 minutes, we stopped and asked for directions several times on the way and each person we asked looked at him, shook their heads dolefully and said "It's a long way", implying that we should have stayed at home or caught a taxi.

Eventually we spotted the underpass in the distance, it was one of those daunting looking fixtures with steep stairs disappearing into a dark cavern that looked as if it was waiting to swallow us whole.

"Are you sure you're up to this" I asked my poor suffering man. He glared at me and said 'I'm not going back now" in that voice I know so well. The one that tells me to shut up before he attacks me with his stick. I took a deep breath and plunged downward.

On reaching the barely lit underpass at the bottom of many stairs we were met with a deep pool of water and a grubby sign naming the roads we could reach once we had escaped the dungeon. None of these was the road we wanted.

We managed to find our way out eventually and discovered West End Music, a delightful shop with a fine owner who bought my book. We will definitely be back once Peter has had his operation.

Stumbling out of the shop tired and thirsty, we spotted a welcoming looking Portuguese cafe on the other side of a busy road. I set off at a run and thought Peter was behind me but when I turned round it was to see him trip and put out his arms to stop himself falling onto the knee that had already been replaced.

Suddenly the pavement was full of people helping him up, bringing out a chair and generally fussing over him. We helped him into the cafe where the kind owners, Bella and Jose, made sure he was alright, finding us a table and bringing welcoming cups of coffee.

Peter and Bella bonded over being Aquarians and Jose refused to take any money for our drinks, these are two of the most delightful people I have ever met who turned a rather frightening event into a bit of a party and it made our day.

The Portuguese cafe opposite West End Music is called the Bicafe, it is wonderful, go there as soon as you can and soak up the atmosphere. The food looked delicious although we didn't really feel up to sampling it this time, but the coffee was outstanding and on a grey cold day the cafe was warm and homely.

We could have stayed all day drinking coffee and chatting to our new friends but it was a long walk back to the park and ride bus stop and we needed to get moving before Peter's bad leg seized up altogether.

We will be back when things are easier for him and this time we will get our wallets out!

On our return journey, which was much slower but less eventful thank goodness, I couldn't help noticing the depressing little piles of personal belongings indicating the presence of homeless people. Blankets and old clothes were heaped up on the pavement, inadequately covered with plastic sheeting against the cold relentless February rain.

Unkempt men huddled around an outdoor food vendor, all clutching mugs and dragging on cigarettes. They spoke loudly amongst themselves and there was an air of camaraderie, as if this group were looking out for one another.

I hope that is the case, I always think one of the saddest aspects of homelessness is the loneliness on the faces of those set apart from society. It's hard to know what to do for the best, we sometimes buy a pack of sandwiches to give out, it doesn't help much but at least it can't do any harm.

We came away from Ipswich strangely moved by our experiences, it hadn't been what we expected in many ways, and we won't be recommending it on TripAdvisor, but then we didn't recommend Barcelona either. Let people find out for themselves.

These events took place on 25th February and less than a month later all the places mentioned here closed, including the beautiful new bookshop Dial Lane Books which had only just opened. I'm so glad I armed myself with some books to see me through lockdown, and also thanks to the owner Andrew Marsh who donated money to the NHS in exchange for copies of my books.

We look forward to repeating this day when lockdown eases and we will once more be looking up, but hopefully not falling down.

Lockdown Stories

Once we were in lockdown I had to look around for new diversions to keep me occupied, no more games of boules or cosy evenings singing with our friends in tiny crowded hostelries for us.

 No more sampling local food in the markets and food fayres famous in these parts, we were on our own indoors- a strange and very different new life for all of us.

In order to escape the never ending doom on the TV and radio I did things I would never have considered before, and even came to enjoy them, some more than others.

I hope you enjoy my musings and can identify with the need to grab hold of anything, no matter how strange, to keep sane in insane times.

PUZZLED

My husband celebrated a big birthday in January and along with his expensive, glamorous presents of theatre tickets and a night in a posh London hotel there was a large, mysterious box from our daughter. She advised him to open it last and said she had bought it as a joke.

It turned out to be the best present she could have bought, a fiendishly difficult 1000 piece jigsaw puzzle called "Retro Records".

Two months later and here we are shut up in our house desperate for diversion and fighting for possession of the precious pieces.

Day 1 was spent finding all the edges, oh the excitement when a corner was discovered, gold star for that one! Then disaster, the frame was complete except for two pieces- out came the box again as we rifled through the contents for the elusive two and then hooray, found them, we could do something else now. I voted to open the wine.

Day 2 and we were working in tandem. The puzzle was a 1960s style record shop with vinyl and posters on the walls with lots of happy browsing customers definitely not practising any social distancing.

Oh the excitement as we traded Jimmy Hendrix' hair for Twiggy's eyelashes. Heard today that the lockdown could last thirteen weeks. We're going to need it.

We started at the top with the groovy album covers. There was a random Elvis who turned out to be Don Williams trying to bamboozle us into thinking he was the King of Rock and Roll and as for the Monkees, hey hey, there's too many of them and their faces are all blurred. And how many Rolling Stones records dotted around the shop, they all look the same, it's driving us mad but we must finish it, we must!

We started with a cunning plan, I would do the top and husband would do the bottom and we would hopefully meet in the middle but we failed to stick to the rules, we kept straying into each others' territory with a blue piece here and an orange piece there, is that Herman's Hermits or The Doors?. Funny how they all look the same when cut out of pieces of cardboard.

Oh no it's Doris Day, where did she come from? I thought it was Dusty Springfield, the hair is exactly the same.

Once we had completed the record sleeves and posters there were still all the customers to assemble. Why are they all wearing identical blue jeans? And blue shirts, surely that wasn't a 60s look, where are all the lovely bells and beads and kaftans or was that the 70s? We're losing the plot.

And a dog, what's that all about? Oh, it's the little dog from the "His Master's Voice" adverts, very funny folks, now is that a lead or part of someone's handbag? Honestly, it's a whole new world of frustration and grief.

We felt quite at a loss when the puzzle was finally completed, when after a moment of sheer panic as we were unable to locate the final piece and I crawled under the table and triumphantly retrieved it and slotted it into place to cheers from a relieved husband,

We contemplated our achievement with pride and I even took a picture to show off on FaceBook, but I am doing this with every tiny event of my life now, sorry friends and family but it's the only way I'm keeping sane lately.

The completed puzzle remained, taking up most of our dining table for several days as we couldn't bring ourselves to take it apart and put it back in it's box. Then I had a message from a friend in our village saying she had seen the picture and had a neighbour who was self- isolating and would like something to keep her occupied, could she please borrow our puzzle as it looked lovely?

At first I was delighted, a new home for our friend, we could have our table back and the puzzle would be of use to someone in their isolation.

I sat down to dismantle the 1000 pieces and found myself suddenly in tears. This happens a lot lately, it can be any little tiny thing, a dripping tap, running out of tins of tomatoes, a TV advert showing a happy Italian family hugging and laughing over plates of spaghetti. I can't cry over tens of thousands of people dying of a vile disease but show me a picture of a dad and his daughter singing together in their kitchen and I'm in bits. Strange days indeed.

My husband agreed that Retro Records was now a member of our family and we couldn't part with it, so I rang my village friend and said we would be happy to lend our puzzle out but we definitely wanted it back, with all the pieces intact.

She was happy to agree to this so we carefully pulled apart our creation, boxed it up and I took it round. Our friend was getting into her car when I arrived so I shouted from 2 metres away that I would leave the parcel on her step. We then wished each other well and went our separate ways, as friends now do.

My husband and I look forward to getting his precious present back one day when this terrible time is over, and putting it back together once more, for old times' sake.

My Limescale lament

I recently joined one of those cleaning groups

on FaceBook, you know the ones, they promise to solve all your cleaning dilemmas without judging you for the filthy beast you really are.

I am now completely obsessed with it, my cupboards bulge with cleaning sprays and gadgets, each one bigger and smellier than the last.

Where I used to buy face creams and cleansers in the belief that they would make me look younger (they're rubbish, I'm ancient and I look it but boy am I moist and fragrant) I now buy cleaning products in the hope that they will rid my house of limescale.

Here where we live in deepest rural Suffolk the limescale problem is on an industrial level. You can't move on our narrow country lanes for big shiny cars driven by rich people rushing to install water softeners in our furry homes. We had an estimate, it would cost us £1200. £1200!!!

For that sort of money I could look like Julia Roberts, including the teeth.

But back to my lovely new friends the sprays, powders and tins, the cloths and scourers, all promising a gleaming limescale free life for my poor crusty house. When we moved in 7 years ago everything sparkled, now it is coated in scale so thick in places it looks like a home for washed-up barnacles. Even the FaceBook group have failed me, I tried all their suggestions and gave myself housemaids knee and aged cracked hands yet still my taps and shower heads have a thin, or not so thin, layer of salt like codfish in those weird recipes you only see on Masterchef. Help!!

I dream of finding a solution one day, of wandering into a dusty forgotten Bargain Store and coming across El Dorado in a Magnum sized bottle of industrial strength cleaner for £1, or two for £1.99. It will smell of Miss Dior, the spray will work first time and I will liberally coat all the crusty surfaces of my house before booking myself into a luxury Spa hotel for the weekend and firmly closing the door.

When I return I will be greeted by sparkling clean, limescale free surfaces that will smell better than my hotel retreat. Everything will be like new again, I will peer into a spotless mirror and Julia Roberts will smile back at me with gleaming abundant perfect teeth.

Feeling Seedy

After tying myself in knots with jigsaw puzzles and using up obscene levels of cleaning products, I have found myself a more gentle and healthy form of recreation-gardening.

 I could always find something more interesting to do before, like re-folding the tea towels, but now I find myself increasingly reading seed catalogues and following keen gardeners on Instagram.

 I've noticed that my TV viewing habits have undergone a distinct change of direction as well, where once you would find me glued to an edgy thriller like Broadchurch or Killing Eve, or an all-out action series like the wonderful Line of Duty, now the highlight of my viewing week is " grow your own at home with Alan Titchmarsh", filmed on a wobbly video recorder by his charming wife Alison in their amazing garden.

Then there's the glorious " Gardener's World". Is it ok to have a crush on Monty Don(I swear it's the hat)? Or to weep like a baby when his dog died?

I've also become fixated on Springwatch with the beavers and ospreys. Oh how I long to see a pine marten, I keep binoculars handy around the house in case one should appear on the wild bank behind our little garden, but so far all I've spotted has been a muntjac deer and the neighbours' cats.

Springwatch this year has inspired me to try to create a wildflower meadow in the corner of our plot. Never mind that we live on a 2012 housing estate built on a former scrap yard-I'm sure I've uncovered a few Jaguars and Renault 5s on my adventures with a spade, never mind, nothing that several wheelbarrows full of expensive topsoil won't solve.

Our garden measures around 40 square feet and faces North East, so swathes of poppies waving in the breeze will be a challenge but when I find myself doubting the wisdom of my ambitions I ask myself " What would Chris Packham do"?

Why, he'd get out a large sheet of graph paper, that's what he'd do, and start plotting.

Next spring, just you wait, we'll be in the National Garden Scheme and coaches will be queuing around our little close with hordes of gardening enthusiasts keen to admire our host of golden dandelions. At least I can stop weeding now.

I've also started buying gardening supplies on the Internet after a confusing and stressful trip to our newly organised local garden centre.

I did try to stick to all the social distancing tapes and arrows but I found myself distracted by the wonderful array of gardening merchandise on offer. I never knew there were so many different types of compost and before I knew it, oh no, another person is heading my way. I found myself doing the 2 metre shuffle before abandoning my quest for the perfect compost and heading into Wildflower Seeds.

Honestly I don't know who is profiting from the sale of wildflower seeds but they must all be billionaires. Have you seen the contents of those posh packets? It's like a pinch of snuff and must cost more per gram than crack cocaine.

The seeds are so small you have to hold your breath when tipping them into your palm or your precious flowers will disappear into the nettles and there's another £2.99 gone west.

Perhaps I'll invest in some tomato feed instead, blood bone and seaweed, that should do the trick. Oh no, there's a pesky person heading my way, I'm off before the Covid Police appear. It's all too stressful, I'm off to fire up the Internet, at least I'll escape my stalker.

I'm not good with technology, it's a well known fact. My family hide when I buy a new gadget as they know I'm about to corner the more tech-savvy amongst them and beg for help.

What's this button for, why do my texts keep disappearing and what on earth did I set as a password?

I'm usually saved by one of the younger grandchildren, they don't think I'm senile, they think I'm cute. For now!

I always said I wouldn't shop online but this virus has

forced me onboard and I'm beginning to enjoy it. The choice is staggering. The other night I spent over an hour looking at wheelbarrows and I didn't even buy one, probably because we've already got one but the online offers are so enticing.

In the end I bought a vegetable trug, well it's a window box come planter really but you've got to start somewhere.

I've bought some tiny lettuces and a few trays of broccoli to go in it. And some tomatoes, well lots of tomatoes plus a pack of radishes. Perhaps I'll order another trug. I wonder what Alan Titchmarsh would do?

One of the saddest of our lockdown losses has been going to the White Horse in Sweffling, which I will state now is my favourite place in the world along with the people who run it. When the doors closed I shed quite a few tears but my main worry was for their most regular customer, a lovely man who lives on his own and spends his evenings in his local safe and happy talking to his friends.

An arrangement is now in place whereby the landlady takes beer round to his house and leaves it outside with letters and cards from his friends as he isn't on the internet. When I heard about this splendid idea I composed a little verse to hopefully make him smile and with luck we can all get together again soon.

Who Cares

Who cares if your hair turns grey

Who cares if you've showered today

Who cares if your clothes are clean

Who cares if you live on beans

Sit in the garden

Watch the bees

Don't mow your lawn

Or trim your trees.

Read a book

Drink more beer

Don't turn on the news

It's too sad to hear.

Write a novel

Take up sport

Don't have a party

You might get caught

By the Covid Police

They know your sort.

But..............

Who cares if you dance all night

On your own

Out of sight

Sing if you want to

Make a din

This isolation's not such a bad thing.

Me and the bees and the trees

During my daily walks to break the monotony of lockdown fever I discovered areas I had never visited before in my own remote rural village. No one else seemed to go there either so I came to look on them as my personal places. It was a huge comfort to me just to walk on my own for hours and let my mind settle.

This little poem came to me on a very warm still day when all I could hear was the hum of the bees, it was a very special moment.

My sandals slap on dusty roads

The only sound I hear

Butterflies swoop through banks of flowers

In the greening fields there are deer

And I walk for miles to still my mind

From thoughts of feared disease

Down quiet lanes through a tunnel of green

Just me and the bees and the trees.

It's getting hotter every day

The farmers long for rain

Tractors toil through clouds of dust

And I walk alone again.

I haven't seen my family

Since frost was on the ground

My friends a distant memory

They mustn't come around.

We used to sing together

Now I hear them on my phone

The songs are still the same

But we're all singing on our own.

So I walk to keep my sanity

Through trees and dust and heat

And mostly I feel happy to be healthy and complete.

Surrounded by the birdsong I never heard before

I join them in my head

Til I'm not lonely anymore.

Lopsided

If like me you have been avoiding mirrors for the last
few months and finding that you no longer recognise
friends and neighbours under their wild and tousled
hair you will appreciate my dilemma as my crowning
glory becomes increasingly peculiar.

Have you lopped off your locks during lockdown?

Although I swore not to give in

It's been seventeen weeks and I look like a freak

It's caused me to break out the gin.

I found me some scissors to work with

They've been handy for toenails and string

I'm sure when it comes to my straggly fringe

They'll turn out to be just the thing.

I looked at tutorials on YouTube

Don't cut it wet, they all said

Chop into the hair, but remember take care

Not to chop up your eyeballs instead.

These scissors are terribly pointy

But I've started so best carry on

I won't tackle the back, just my long fringe to hack

Oh help, where've the plasters all gone?

My eyeballs remain where they should be

But I can't say the same for my hair.

It still hangs round my face and it looks a disgrace

I'm riddled with shame and despair.

I'm off to the hairdresser shortly

In my mask and my apron and gown.

On the 25th day of July at midday

Then I'll be the talk of the town.

This piece is for all those people called Janet, Jane or Pat. Or Reg, Sid or John, who wish their unimaginative parents had tried that little bit harder.

WHAT's IN A NAME

Do you ever find yourself longing for a more exciting or glamorous title than the one handed to you by your parents? Something exotic and challenging to pronounce, something to impress your friends and colleagues? Something with more than one syllable?

I suffered a serious bout of name envy recently whilst watching the early evening news and coming across an impassioned speech by the sister of Jacob Rees- Mogg. She waved her arms dramatically in the air (the woman has no shame) and cried out "My name is Annunziata Rees-Mogg!!"

I was stunned- five syllables and all those lovely vowels, it's not a name it's a proclamation.

My name is Sue. Not a proclamation but a comic song about a father who humiliates his poor son by naming him after me. My name is Sue, how do you do, now you're going to die. Oh dear...

I looked up Annunziata, it refers to the virgin Mary receiving news from the Angel Gabriel that she was to become the mother of Christ. Susan means Lily, life just ain't fair, a view shared by my husband Peter whose name means a rock.

I have a strange obsession with our much maligned Leader of the House of Commons and his penchant for awarding his children fantastical epithets. The six lucky recipients have at least three forenames apiece and each includes the kind of strange romantic choices I can only dream about.

Amongst Jacob's choices (surely his wife has nothing to do with these, a mother wouldn't be so cruel) are Anselm, Pius, Boniface, Sixtus and my own personal favourite, Wulfric.

Now that is a name that comes with its own Asbo, surely something you would call a Viking marauder. Wulfric the grim, King of the mean and scary tribe. Apparently the original Wulfric was a hermit saint born in 1080, a lot of the Rees-Mogg brood bear the names of saints, they probably eat all their greens too.

I was disappointed to learn that the long-suffering Mrs Rees-Mogg doesn't want any more children. What a spoil sport! There are so many weird and wonderful names still to be inflicted, I mean bestowed, on future mini Moggs, and I have recently invented a brilliant new game to occupy those sleepless nights when I am lying awake wondering if I have Covid 19. It's hard to sleep with a thermometer wedged under your arm and playing Name that Mogg is a great distraction.

There are a few rules to follow, the names must be ridiculous, more than one syllable in length and sound as if they could be Latin. They should come in pairs and be themed, thus;

Illnesses: Scarlettina and Impetigo

Embarrassing illnesses: Diarrhoea and Halitosis

Scandalous Illnesses: Chlamydia and Gonorrhoea

Or for an unhappy quartet you could add Syphillis and Herpes.

Alternatively, if you feel a little culture is called for, there are some magnificent examples in Shakespeare: Cordelia and Goneril (please don't confuse the poor girl with Gonorrhoea, we're in enough trouble as it is)

Malvolio and Mercutio

Proteus and Publias

Pyramus and Thisbee

Or lastly my favourite category, the spells of Harry Potter:

Who wouldn't want to be called Alohomora, a handy name for a Rees- Mogg this as it is a spell for opening doors.

Or Sectumsempra, a curse causing a cut that never heals which seems rather extreme even for a Rees-Mogg.

Or how about Wingardian Leviosa, a spell to cause objects to levitate, great fun at parties, not so good at funerals.

Come on Mrs Rees-Mogg, your country needs you, give us another one do.

Once more down to the
beach, with friends

When lockdown started one of the things I missed most was being able to meet up and sing along with our many friends.

We moved to Suffolk in 2013 to start a new life, not knowing what that new life would bring, and one of the greatest and most surprising joys I discovered was the huge singing community scattered throughout the rural Suffolk villages and their tradition of gathering together to perform in remote and ancient pubs.

We are not a choir, but groups of people brought together by our love of old folk songs and rustic instruments which we play with varying degrees of ability but equal amounts of enormous enthusiasm.

One group was organised by our good friend Doris the German barmaid who you can read about in my previous collection of stories called "Come in at random in any key you like".

Doris calls her motley collection of performers " The Desperadoes" and I consider it an honour to be a member.

I myself don't play a musical instrument, unless you count the triangle or tambourine, but I sing gamely with the rest and have a talent for remembering the words of obscure songs dating back to days before I was born, a frighteningly long time ago.

We started out playing in the back room at the Royal Standard in Leiston then graduated to the Football Association hall and from there moved a year ago to the White Horse, also in Leiston, where our numbers were growing nicely until this pandemic struck.

The members of the Desperadoes vary in age and state of health, you could almost call us a support group as we lift each other through the ill health and loss that comes with our stage of life, but we would be no match for Covid 19.

 At the beginning of March we gathered in the White Horse for the last time, not knowing when or if we would sing together again. It was a very emotional occasion and when we went our separate ways we hugged each other goodbye, not knowing that hugging would from now on be forbidden and taboo.

 We sang "We'll meet again" and "Que sera, sera" and finally our theme song, "Forever Young", and as I hunted for my hankies I saw many others wiping away tears too.

We then got in our cars and went back to our quiet homes. We were not to see each other again for four long months.

Towards the end of June, as lockdown was slowly

easing, Doris began to contact members of the Desperadoes again to see how we felt about meeting up. It wouldn't be possible to use the White Horse, which along with all our other lovely Suffolk pubs was sadly still closed, but perhaps it would work to come together outside in a quiet area with plenty of space.

The place she suggested was Sizewell Beach. There is a cafe called Sizewell Tea (because it is situated next to the car park at Sizewell C, the nuclear power station, cue lots of jokes about green tea and glow in the dark bacon sandwiches) and above the car park is a quiet area backing onto woods which could be suitable for a band of minstrels to gather together.

The Desperdoes felt rather nervous about this, was it even legal, would we have to come in disguise and bring gettaway cars, but Doris assured us that as long as we kept a good social distance and didn't get over excited and hug each other she couldn't forsee any problems.

We needed a lot of reassurance, being rather timid Desperadoes, but in the end the bolder amongst us decided it was worth the risk and a date was set for the 12th of July. I pencilled in the date on my calendar. It was the first entry since March and stood out from the long empty weeks like a star in the dark sky. I was VERY happy.

The days leading up to our meeting were filled with rehearsals, research and weather-watching. We drew up a tentative list of songs to perform, nothing too strenuous or over-emotional, keep it light, keep it happy. Messages appeared daily on our FaceBook group page and the list of willing participants grew longer. This was really going to happen!

The weather that Sunday was perfect, after a rather cold and blowy week the sun shone with confidence and there was only a little high cloud. I put on a jaunty pair of shorts and my sparkly sandals, a floaty top and some festive dangly earrings and we were off. The fleeces and woolly hat could stay in the car....

On arrival at the beach we soon spotted our long lost and much missed buddies clutching their precious instruments and word sheets, so we refrained from hugging them and took up our positions 2 metres away from the nearest person next to the makeshift stage.

Doris and her fellow partner in crime Brian had done us proud with a taped-off area for the performers complete with bunting and a table for spare instruments and essentials like beer and crisps. The sun shone and the gulls called, there was excitement in the air.

Doris took the stage first with her new song, a 2020 version of "Streets of London" called "Streets of Leiston". Our Doris is the mistress of the sad song and this awful year has given her plenty of material, especially as she works for the pharmacy in Leiston and sees at first hand the devastation the virus has caused in her small community.

This was followed by a lively version of "That's all right now Mama" which had us all out of our seats doing some distanced dancing.

We were now drawing a small crowd of onlookers who clapped politely but looked a little bemused, Sizewell isn't famed for its music festivals but there was a festive feeling in the air that none of us had experienced since March.

Our turn came round far too quickly and Peter and I performed our signature tune, "Colours" by Donovan, accompanied by Doris on her faithful guitar. We followed this with "San Francisco Bay" and "Frankie and Johnnie" then we flopped back into our beach chairs and let the other Desperadoes take the stage.

The gulls joined in and people walking their dogs stopped to watch the fun, some wag called out "Hello Sizewellbury!!" and the party was underway.

All the old favourites came out, Delilah was there with Peggy Sue and Lucille, and a lovely time was had by all, including One Song George who came along especially to give us his famous version of "They tried to tell us we're too young" which he had re written in celebration of a late life love and entitled "They tried to tell us we're too old".

The most moving moment came when one of our oldest members walked onto the stage and sang "We'll meet again". This song always makes me tearful and on this occasion I was not the only one fumbling for a tissue. It was dawning on all of us that we stood to lose something unique and precious if this virus is not defeated, there will be no impromtu outside performances once the dreaded winter sets in and many of our members who live alone must have been wondering what the future has in store for them. I hope and pray it is not the awful loneliness brought on by isolation and lockdown.

After a lovely afternoon of joyous singing, dancing and laughter Doris brought our party to an end with her traditional medley of "Three Little Birds", "Dirty Old Town" and "Forever Young".

For two glorious hours we had escaped the shadow of coronavirus, our happy band had enjoyed a small taste of normality and the companionship singing old familiar songs brings.

It was hard to part in this way, no physical contact, only promises to repeat the experience if the virus, and the weather, allow. We waved sadly at each other and watched our friends drift away clutching   their guitars, ukuleles and empty beer bottles.

Peter and I drove quietly back to our small village some twenty miles from Sizewell.

 Suffolk is a large and spread-out county and many of our friends only meet up to sing together. We may not know when, but do know where we'll all meet again.